HOOD WINKED

HOOD WINKED

Poems by Thomas Hood

Illustrated by Pavel Büchler

1982

CHATTO & WINDUS

LONDON

Published by
Chatto & Windus Ltd
40 William IV Street
London WC2N 4DF

Clarke, Irwin & Co., Ltd
Toronto

British Library
Cataloguing in Publication Data
Hood, Thomas
Hood winked
I. Title
822'.7 PR4800.H2

ISBN 0 7011 2626 4

Illustrations © Pavel Büchler 1982

Typeset by Inforum Ltd, Portsmouth
Printed in Great Britain by
Redwood Burn Ltd., Trowbridge, Wiltshire,
and bound by Mansell Bookbinders Ltd
Witham, Essex

CONTENTS

SALLY SIMPKIN'S LAMENT
OR, JOHN JONES'S KIT-CAT-ASTROPHE

'Oh! what is that comes gliding in,
    And quite in middling haste?
It is the picture of my Jones,
    And painted to the waist.

'It is not painted to the life,
    For where's the trousers blue?
Oh Jones, my dear! – Oh dear! my Jones,
    What is become of you?'

'Oh! Sally dear, it is too true, –
    The half that you remark
Is come to say my other half
    Is bit off by a shark!

'Oh! Sally, sharks do things by halves,
    Yet most completely do!
A bite in one place seems enough,
    But I've been bit in two.

'You know I once was all your own,
    But now a shark must share!
But let that pass – for now to you
    I'm neither here nor there.

'Alas! death has a strange divorce
    Effected in the sea,
It has divided me from you,
    And even you from me!

'Don't fear my ghost will walk of nights
    To haunt as people say;

7

My ghost *can't* walk, for, oh! my legs
   Are many leagues away!

'Lord! think when I am swimming round,
   And looking where the boat is,
A shark just snaps away a *half*,
   Without "a *quarter*'s notice".

'One half is here, the other half
   Is near Columbia placed;
Oh! Sally, I have got the whole
   Atlantic for my waist.

'But now, adieu – a long adieu!
   I've solved death's awful riddle,
And would say more, but I am doomed
   To break off in the middle.'

FRENCH AND ENGLISH

Never go to France
Unless you know the lingo,
If you do, like me,
You will repent, by jingo.
Staring like a fool,
And silent as a mummy,
There I stood alone,
A nation with a dummy:

Chaises stand for chairs,
They christen letters *Billies*,
They call their mothers *mares*,
And all their daughters *fillies*;
Strange it was to hear,
I'll tell you what's a good 'un,
They call their leather *queer*,
And half their shoes are wooden.

Signs I had to make
For every little notion,
Limbs all going like
A telegraph in motion,
For wine I reeled about,
To show my meaning fully,
And made a pair of horns,
To ask for 'beef and bully'.

Moo! I cried for milk;
I got my sweet things snugger,
When I kissed Jeanette,
'Twas understood for sugar.
If I wanted bread,
My jaws I set a-going,

And asked for new-laid eggs,
By clapping hands and crowing!

If I wished a ride,
I'll tell you how I got it;
On my stick astride
I made believe to trot it;
Then their cash was strange,
It bored me every minute,
Now here's a *hog* to change,
How many *sows* are in it!

Never go to France,
Unless you know the lingo;
If you do, like me,
You will repent, by jingo;
Staring like a fool,
And silent as a mummy,
There I stood alone,
A nation with a dummy!

Billies: *billets*
mares: *mères*
fillies: *filles*
queer: *cuir*
hog: Old English slang term for shilling
sows: *sous* (French coin)

I REMEMBER, I REMEMBER

I remember, I remember,
The house where I was born,
The little window where the sun
Came peeping in at morn;
He never came a wink too soon,
Nor brought too long a day,
But now, I often wish the night
Had borne my breath away!

I remember, I remember,
The roses, red and white,
The violets, and the lily-cups,
Those flowers made of light!
The lilacs where the robin built,
And where my brother set
The laburnum on his birth-day, —
The tree is living yet!

I remember, I remember,
Where I was used to swing,
And thought the air must rush as fresh
To swallows on the wing;
My spirit flew in feathers then,
That is so heavy now,
And summer pools could hardly cool
The fever on my brow!

I remember, I remember,
The fir trees dark and high;
I used to think their slender tops
Were close against the sky:

It was a childish ignorance,
But now 'tis little joy
To know I'm farther off from heaven
Than when I was a boy.

THE SAUSAGE-MAKER'S GHOST
A LONDON LEGEND

Somewhere in Leather Lane —
  I wonder that it was not Mincing,
  And for this reason most convincing,
    That Mr Brain
Dealt in those well-minced cartridges of meat
  Some people like to eat —
However, all such quibbles overstepping,
In Leather Lane he lived; and drove a trade
In porcine sausages, though London made,
    Called 'Epping'.

    Right brisk was the demand,
Seldom his goods stayed long on hand,
For out of all adjacent courts and lanes
  Young Irish ladies and their swains,
  Such soups of girls and broths of boys!
    Sought his delicious chains,
  Preferred to all polonies, saveloys,
    And other foreign toys —
    The mere chance passengers
    Who saw his 'sassengers',
      Of sweetness undeniable,
  So sleek, so mottled, and so friable,
Stepped in, forgetting every other thought,
    And bought.

    Meanwhile a constant thumping
Was heard, a sort of subterranean chumping —
    Incessant was the noise
But though he had a foreman and assistant,
  With all the tools consistent,
(Besides a wife and two fine chopping boys)

His means were not yet vast enough
        For chopping fast enough
To meet the call from streets, and lanes, and passages,
        For first-chop 'sassages'.

        However, Mr Brain
Was none of those dull men and slow,
Who, flying bird-like by a railway train,
Sigh for the heavy mails of long ago;
He did not set his face 'gainst innovations
        For rapid operations,
And therefore in a kind of waking dream
Listened to some hot-water sprite that hinted
To have his meat chopp'd, as the *Times* was printed,
        By steam!

        Accordingly in happy-hour,
A bran-new Engine went to work
    Chopping up pounds on pounds of pork
With all the energy of Two-Horse-Power,
        And wonderful celerity –
When lo! when every thing to hope responded,
Whether his head was turned by his prosperity,
Whether he had some sly intrigue, in verity,
        The man absconded!

        His anxious Wife in vain
        Placarded Leather Lane,
And all the suburbs with descriptive bills,
Such as are issued when from homes and tills
Clerks, dogs, cats, lunatics, and children roam;
Besides advertisements in all the journals,
        Or weeklies or diurnals,
        Beginning 'LEFT HIS HOME' –

The sausage-maker, spite of white and black,
        Never came back.

Never, alive! – But on the seventh night,
Just when the yawning grave its dead releases,
    Filling his bedded Wife with sore affright
        In walked his grisly Sprite,
        In fifty thousand pieces!
    'O Mary!' so it seemed
In hollow melancholy tones to say,
Whilst thro' its airy shape the moonlight gleamed
    With scarcely dimmer ray –
'O Mary! let your hopes no longer flatter,
Prepare at once to drink of sorrow's cup, –
    It ain't no use to mince the matter –
        The Engine's chopped me up!

polonies, saveloys: two kinds of sausage

ON THE DEATH OF THE GIRAFFE

They say, God wot!
She died upon the spot:
But then in spots she was so rich, –
I wonder which?

THE SUB-MARINE

It was a brave and jolly wight,
   His cheek was baked and brown,
For he had been in many climes
   With captains of renown,
And fought with those who fought so well
   At Nile and Camperdown.

His coat it was a soldier coat,
   Of red with yellow faced,
But (merman-like) he looked marine
   All downward from the waist;
His trousers were so wide and blue,
   And quite in sailor taste!

He put the rummer to his lips,
   And drank a jolly draught;
He raised the rummer many times —
   And ever as he quaffed,
The more he drank, the more the ship
   Seemed pitching fore and aft!

The ship seemed pitching fore and aft,
   As in a heavy squall;
It gave a lurch and down he went,
   Head-foremost in his fall!
Three times he did not rise, alas!
   He never rose at all!

But down he went, right down at once,
   Like any stone he dived,
He could not see, or hear, or feel —
   Of senses all deprived!

At last he gave a look around
　　To see where he arrived!

And all that he could see was green,
　　Sea-green on every hand!
And then he tried to sound beneath,
　　And all he felt was sand!
There he was fain to lie, for he
　　Could neither sit nor stand!

And lo! above his head there bent
　　A strange and staring lass!
One hand was in her yellow hair,
　　The other held a glass;
A mermaid she must surely be
　　If ever mermaid was!

Her fish-like mouth was opened wide,
　　Her eyes were blue and pale,
Her dress was of the ocean green,
　　When ruffled by a gale;
Thought he, 'Beneath that petticoat
　　She hides a salmon-tail!'

She look'd as siren ought to look,
　　A sharp and bitter shrew,
To sing deceiving lullabies
　　For mariners to rue, —
But when he saw her lips apart,
　　It chill'd him through and through!

With either hand he stopped his ears
　　Against her evil cry;
Alas, alas, for all his care,
　　His doom it seemed to die,

Her voice went ringing through his head,
    It was so sharp and high!

He thrust his fingers farther in
    At each unwilling ear,
But still, in very spite of all,
    The words were plain and clear;
'I can't stand here the whole day long
    To hold your glass of beer!'

With opened mouth and opened eyes,
    Up rose the Sub-marine,
And gave a stare to find the sands
    And deeps where he had been:
There was no siren with her glass!
    No waters ocean-green!

The wet deception from his eyes
    Kept fading more and more,
He only saw the bar-maid stand
    With pouting lip before –
The small green parlour of The Ship,
    And little sanded floor!

NO!

No sun – no moon!
No morn – no noon!
No dawn – no dusk – no proper time of day –
No sky – no earthly view –
No distance looking blue –
No road – no street – no 't'other side the way' –
No end to any Row –
No indications where the Crescents go –
No top to any steeple –
No recognitions of familiar people –
No courtesies for showing 'em –
No knowing 'em! –
No travelling at all – no locomotion,
No inkling of the way – no notion –
'No go' – by land or ocean –
No mail – no post –
No news from any foreign coast –
No Park – no Ring – no afternoon gentility –
No company – no nobility –
No warmth, no cheerfulness, no healthful ease,
No comfortable feel in any member –
No shade, no shine, no butterflies, no bees,
No fruits, no flowers, no leaves, no birds, –
November!

DOMESTIC ASIDES;
OR, TRUTH IN PARENTHESES

'I really take it very kind,
This visit, Mrs Skinner!
I have not seen you such an age —
(The wretch has come to dinner!)

'Your daughters, too, what loves of girls —
What heads for painters' easels!
Come here and kiss the infant, dears, —
(And give it p'rhaps the measles!)

'Your charming boys I see are home
From Reverend Mr Russel's;
'Twas very kind to bring them both, —
(What boots for my new Brussels!)

'What! little Clara left at home?
Well now I call that shabby:
I should have loved to kiss her so, —
(A flabby, dabby, babby!)

'And Mr S., I hope he's well,
Ah! though he lives so handy,
He never now drops in to sup, —
(The better for our brandy!)

'Come, take a seat — I long to hear
About Matilda's marriage;
You're come, of course, to spend the day!
(Thank Heav'n, I hear the carriage!)

'What! must you go? next time I hope
You'll give me longer measure;

Nay – I shall see you down the stairs –
(With most uncommon pleasure!)

Good-bye! good-bye! remember all
Next time you'll take your dinners!
(Now, David, mind I'm not at home
In future to the Skinners!)'

FAITHLESS SALLY BROWN

Young Ben he was a nice young man,
   A carpenter by trade;
And he fell in love with Sally Brown,
   That was a lady's maid.

But as they fetched a walk one day,
   They met a press-gang crew;
And Sally she did faint away,
   Whilst Ben he was brought to.

The Boatswain swore with wicked words,
   Enough to shock a saint,
That though she did seem in a fit,
   'Twas nothing but a feint.

'Come girl,' said he, 'hold up your head,
   He'll be as good as me;
For when your swain is in our boat,
   A boatswain he will be.'

So when they'd made their game of her,
   And taken off her elf,
She roused, and found she only was
   A coming to herself.

'And is he gone, and is he gone?'
   She cried, and wept outright:
'Then I will to the water side,
   And see him out of sight.'

A waterman came up to her, –
   'Now, young woman,' said he,

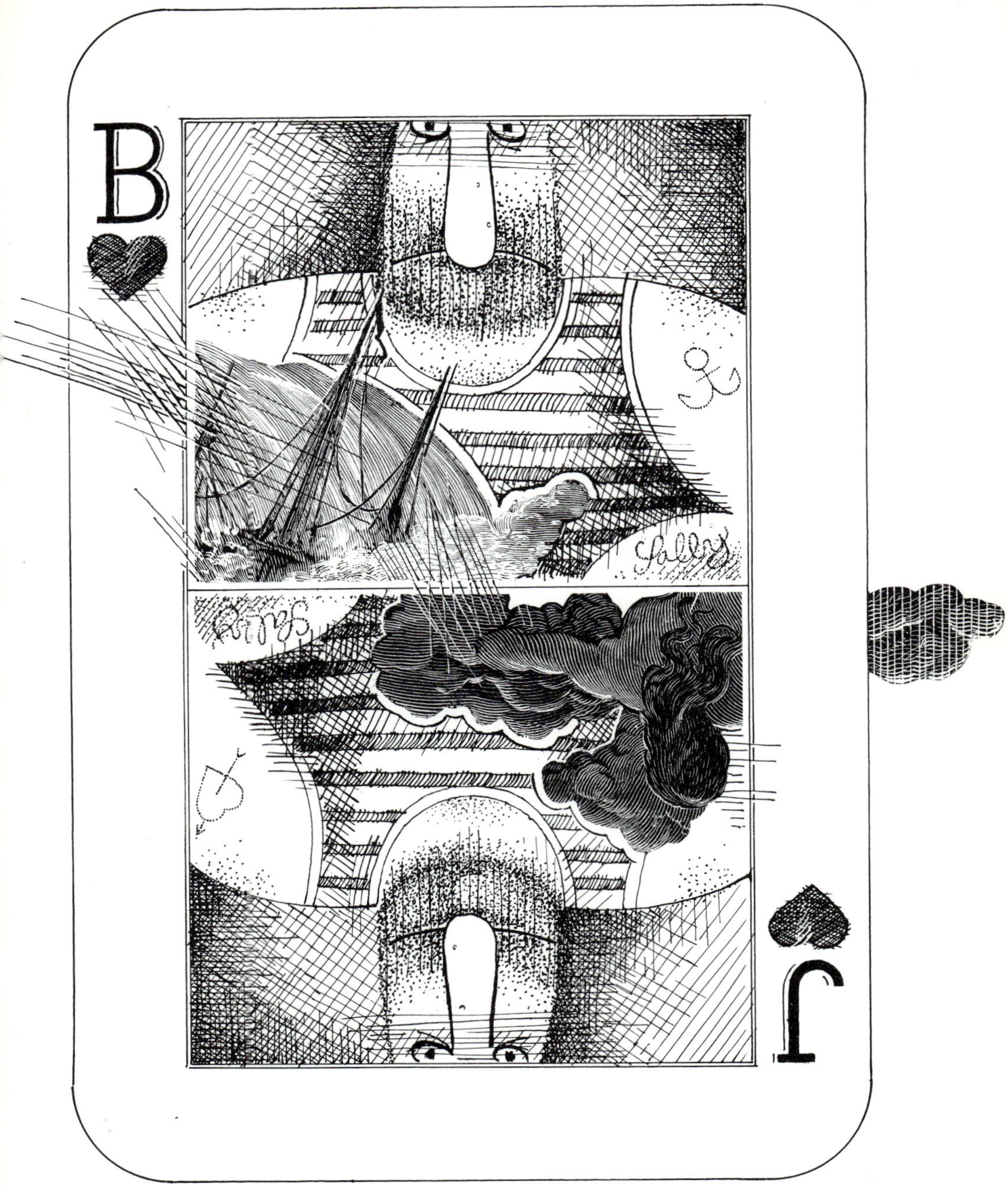
B
J

'If you weep on so, you will make
    Eye-water in the sea.'

'Alas! they've taken my beau Ben
    To sail with old Benbow;'
And her woe began to run afresh,
    As if she'd said Gee woe!

Says he, 'They've only taken him
    To the Tender ship, you see;'
'The Tender-ship,' cried Sally Brown,
    'What a hard-ship that must be!

'O! would I were a mermaid now,
    For then I'd follow him;
But Oh! – I'm not a fish-woman,
    And so I cannot swim.

'Alas! I was not born beneath
    The virgin and the scales,
So I must curse my cruel stars,
    And walk about in Wales.'

Now Ben had sailed to many a place
    That's underneath the world;
But in two years the ship came home
    And all her sails were furled.

But when he called on Sally Brown,
    To see how she went on,
He found she'd got another Ben,
    Whose Christian-name was John.

'O Sally Brown, O Sally Brown,
    How could you serve me so?

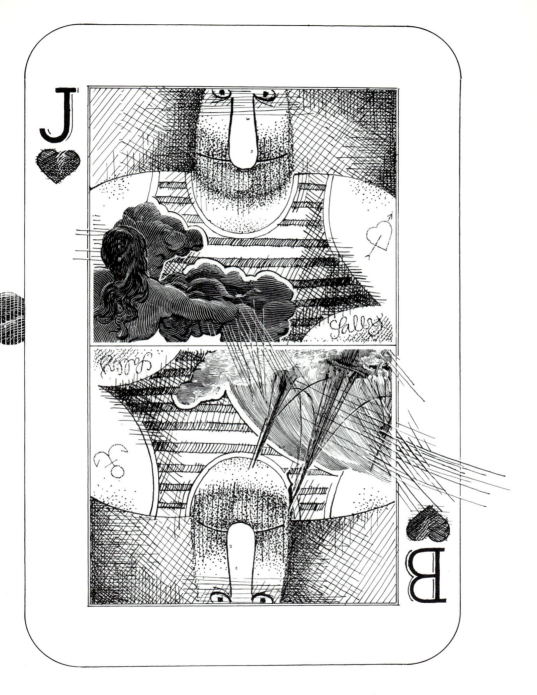

I've met with many a breeze before,
    But never such a blow.'

Then reading on his 'bacco box
    He heaved a bitter sigh,
And then began to eye his pipe,
    And then to pipe his eye.

And then he tried to sing 'All's Well',
    'But could not though he tried;
His head was turned, and so he chewed
    His pigtail till he died.

His death, which happened in his berth,
    At forty-odd befell:
They went and told the sexton, and
    The sexton tolled the bell.

her elf: her young man
pipe his eye: weep

SHE IS FAR FROM THE LAND

Cables entangling her,
Shipspars for mangling her,
Ropes, sure of strangling her;
Blocks over-dangling her;
Tiller to batter her,
Topmast to shatter her,
Tobacco to spatter her;
Boreas blustering,
Boatswain quite flustering,
Thunder-clouds mustering
To blast her with sulphur —
If the deep don't engulf her;
Sometimes fear's scrutiny
Pries out a mutiny,
Sniffs conflagration,
Or hints at starvation: —
All the sea-dangers,
Buccaneers, rangers,
Pirates and Sallee-men,
Algerine galleymen,
Tornadoes and typhons,
And horrible syphons,
And submarine travels
Thro' roaring sea-navels.
Everything wrong enough,
Long-boat not long enough,
Vessel not strong enough;
Pitch marring frippery,
The deck very slippery,
And the cabin — built sloping,

The Captain a-toping,
And the Mate a blasphemer,
That names his Redeemer, —
With inward uneasiness;
The cook known by greasiness,
The victuals beslubber'd,
Her bed — in a cupboard;
Things of strange christening,
Snatched in her listening,
Blue lights and red lights
And mention of dead-lights
And shrouds made a theme of,
Things horrid to dream of, —
And *buoys* in the water
To fear all exhort her;
Her friend no Leander,
Herself no sea-gander,
And ne'er a cork jacket
On board of the packet;
The breeze still a stiffening,
The trumpet quite deafening;
Thoughts of repentance,
And doomsday and sentence;
Everything sinister,
Not a church minister, —
Pilot a blunderer,
Coral reefs under her,
Ready to sunder her;
Trunks tipsy-topsy,
The ship in a dropsy;
Waves oversurging her,
Sirens a-dirgeing her;

Sharks all expecting her,
Sword-fish dissecting her,
Crabs with their hand-vices
Punishing land vices;
Sea-dogs and unicorns,
Things with no puny horns,
Mermen carnivorous –
'Good Lord deliver us!'

Boreas: the north wind
Sallee-men: Moorish pirates
a-toping: drinking heavily
Leander: a Greek youth who swam the Hellespont

OLD BAILEY BALLAD

He has shaved off his whiskers and blackened his
   brows,
Wears a patch and a wig of false hair, —
But it's him — Oh it's him! — we exchanged lovers' vows
When I lived up in Cavendish Square.

He had beautiful eyes, and his lips were the same,
And his voice was soft as a flute —
Like a Lord or a Marquis he looked, when he came
To make love in his master's best suit.

If I lived for a thousand long years from my birth,
I shall never forget what he told;
How he loved me beyond the rich women of earth,
With their jewels and silver and gold!

When he kissed me, and bade me adieu with a sigh,
By the light of the sweetest of moons,
Oh how little I dreamt I was bidding good-bye
To my Missis's tea-pot and spoons!

SKIPPING, A MYSTERY

Little children skip,
The rope so gaily gripping,
  Tom and Harry,
  Jane and Mary,
  Kate, Diana,
  Susan, Anna,
All are fond of skipping!

The Grasshoppers all skip,
The early dew-drop sipping,
  Under, over,
  Bent and clover,
  Daisy, sorrel,
  Without quarrel,
All are fond of skipping!

The tiny Fairies skip,
At midnight softly tripping;
  Puck and Peri,
  Never weary,
  With an antic
  Quite romantic,
All are fond of skipping.

The little Boats they skip,
Beside the heavy Shipping,
  While the squalling
  Winds are calling,
  Falling, rising,
  Rising, falling,
All are fond of skipping!

The pale Diana skips
The silver billows tipping,
  With a dancing
  Lustre glancing
  To the motion
  Of the ocean –
All are fond of skipping!

The very Dogs they skip,
While threatened with a whipping,
  Wheeling, prancing,
  Learning, dancing,
  To a measure,
  What a pleasure!
All are fond of skipping!

The little fleas they skip,
And nightly come a nipping,
  Lord and Lady,
  Jude and Thady,
  In the night
  So dark and shady –
All are fond of skipping!

The autumn leaves they skip;
When blasts the trees are stripping;
  Bounding, whirling,
  Sweeping, twirling,
  And in wanton
  Mazes curling,
All are fond of skipping!

The Apparitions skip,
Some mortal grievance ripping,
  Thorough many
  A crack and cranny,
  And the keyhole
  Good as any –
All are fond of skipping!

But oh! how Readers skip,
In heavy volumes dipping!
  ***** and *****
  **** and *****
  *** and *****
    ****
All are fond of skipping!

bent: stiff grass
Diana: the moon

DECEMBER AND MAY

'Crabbed Age and Youth cannot live together.' — Shakespeare

Said Nestor, to his pretty wife, quite sorrowful one day,
'Why, dearest, will you shed in pearls those lovely eyes away?
You ought to be more fortified.' 'Ah, brute, be quiet, do,
I know I'm not so fortyfied, nor fiftyfied, as you!

'Oh, men are vile deceivers all, as I have ever heard,
You'd die for me you swore, and I – I took you at your word.
I was a tradesman's widow then – a pretty chance I've made;
To live, and die the wife of one, a widower by trade!'

'Come, come, my dear, these flighty airs declare, in sober truth,
You want as much in age, indeed, as I can want in youth;
Besides, you said you liked old men, though now at me you huff.'
'Why, yes,' she said, 'and so I do – but you're not old enough!'

'Come, come, my dear, let's make it up, and have a quiet hive;
I'll be the best of men, – I mean, I'll be the best *alive*!
Your grieving so will kill me, for it cuts me to the core.' –
'I thank ye, sir, for telling me – for now I'll grieve the more!'

A LAY OF REAL LIFE

Who ruined me ere I was born,
Sold every acre, grass or corn,
And left the next heir all forlorn?
     My Grandfather.

Who said my mother was no nurse,
And physicked me and made me worse,
Till infancy became a curse?
     My Grandmother.

Who left me in my seventh year,
A comfort to my mother dear,
And Mr Pope, the overseer?
     My Father.

Who let me starve, to buy her gin,
Till all my bones came through my skin,
Then called me 'ugly little sin?'
     My Mother.

Who said my mother was a Turk,
And took me home – and made me work,
But managed half my meals to shirk?
     My Aunt.

Who 'of all earthly things' would boast,
'He hated others' brats the most,'
And therefore made me feel my post?
     My Uncle.

Who got in scrapes, an endless score,
And always laid them at my door,

Till many a bitter pang I bore?
     My Cousin.

Who took me home when mother died,
Again with father to reside,
Black shoes, clean knives, run far and wide?
     My Stepmother.

Who marred my stealthy urchin joys,
And when I played cried 'What a noise!' —
Girls always hector over boys —
     My Sister.

Who used to share in what was mine,
Or took it all, did he incline,
'Cause I was eight, and he was nine?
     My Brother.

Who stroked my head, and said 'Good lad,'
And gave me sixpence, 'all he had;'
But at the stall the coin was bad?
     My Godfather.

Who, gratis, shared my social glass,
But when misfortune came to pass,
Referr'd me to the pump? Alas!
     My Friend.

Through all this weary world, in brief,
Who ever sympathised with grief,
Or shared my joy — my sole relief?
     Myself.

MARY'S GHOST
A PATHETIC BALLAD

'Twas in the middle of the night,
    To sleep young William tried,
When Mary's ghost came stealing in,
    And stood at his bed-side.

'O William dear! O William dear!
    My rest eternal ceases;
Alas! my everlasting peace
    Is broken into pieces.

'I thought the last of all my cares
    Would end with my last minute;
But tho' I went to my long home,
    I didn't stay long in it.

'The body-snatchers they have come,
    And made a snatch at me;
It's very hard them kind of men
    Won't let a body be!

'You thought that I was buried deep
    Quite decent like and chary,
But from her grave in Mary-bone
    They've come and boned your Mary.

'The arm that used to take your arm
    Is took to Dr Vyse;
And both my legs are gone to walk
    The hospital at Guy's.

'I vowed that you should have my hand,
    But fate gives us denial;

44

You'll find it there, at Dr Bell's,
    In spirits and a phial.

'As for my feet, the little feet
    You used to call so pretty,
There's one, I know, in Bedford Row,
    The t'other's in the city.

'I can't tell where my head is gone,
    But Dr Carpue can:
As for my trunk, it's all packed up
    To go by Pickford's van.

'I wish you'd go to Mr P.
    And save me such a ride;
I don't half like the outside place,
    They've took for my inside.

'The cock it crows – I must be gone!
    My William we must part!
But I'll be yours in death, altho'
    Sir Astley has my heart.

'Don't go to weep upon my grave,
    And think that there I be;
They haven't left an atom there
    Of my anatomie.'

chary: cherished
Mary-bone: Marylebone

EPIGRAM: THE SUPERIORITY OF MACHINERY

A Mechanic his labour will often discard
   If the rate of his pay he dislikes;
But a clock – and its *case* is uncommonly hard –
   Will continue to work though it *strikes*.

A PARENTAL ODE TO MY SON,
AGED THREE YEARS AND FIVE MONTHS

Thou happy, happy elf!
(But stop, – first let me kiss away that tear) –
Thou tiny image of myself!
(My love, he's poking peas into his ear!)
Thou merry, laughing sprite!
With spirits feather-light,
Untouched by sorrow and unsoiled by sin –
(Good heavens! the child is swallowing a pin!)

Thou little tricksy Puck!
With antic toys so funnily bestuck,
Light as the singing bird that wings the air –
(The door! the door! he'll tumble down the stair!)
Thou darling of thy sire!
(Why Jane, he'll set his pinafore a-fire!)
Thou imp of mirth and joy!
In love's dear chain so strong and bright a link,
Thou idol of thy parents – (Drat the boy!
There goes my ink!)

Thou cherub but of earth;
Fit playfellow for Fays, by moonlight pale,
In harmless sport and mirth,
(That dog will bite him if he pulls its tail!)
Thou human humming-bee, extracting honey
From every blossom in the world that blows,
Singing in Youth's Elysium ever sunny –
(Another tumble! – that's his precious nose!)

Thy father's pride and hope!
(He'll break the mirror with that skipping-rope!)
With pure heart newly stamped from Nature's mint –

48

(Where *did* he learn that squint?)
    Thou young domestic dove!
(He'll have that jug off, with another shove!)
  Dear nursling of the hymeneal nest!
   (Are those torn clothes his best!)
    Little epitome of man!
(He'll climb upon the table, that's his plan!)
Touched with the beauteous tints of dawning life —
    (He's got a knife!)

    Thou enviable being!
No storms, no clouds, in thy blue sky foreseeing,
    Play on, play on,
    My elfin John!
Toss the light ball — bestride the stick —
(I knew so many cakes would make him sick!)
With fancies buoyant as the thistledown,
Prompting the face grotesque, and antic brisk,
    With many a lamb-like frisk,
(He's got the scissors, snipping at your gown!)

    Thou pretty opening rose!
(Go to your mother, child, and wipe your nose!)
Balmy, and breathing music like the South,
(He really brings my heart into my mouth!)
Fresh as the morn, and brilliant as its star, —
(I wish that window had an iron bar!)
Bold as the hawk, yet gentle as the dove —
    (I'll tell you what, my love,
I cannot write, unless he's sent above!)

YOUTH AND AGE

Impatient of his childhood,
  'Ah me!' exclaimed young Arthur,
Whilst roving in the wild wood,
  'I wish I were my father!'
Meanwhile, to see his Arthur
  So skip, and play, and run,
'Ah me!' exclaims the father,
  'I wish I were my son!'

FAITHLESS NELLY GRAY
A PATHETIC BALLAD

Ben Battle was a soldier bold,
    And used to war's alarms:
But a cannon-ball took off his legs,
    So he laid down his arms!

Now as they bore him off the field,
    Said he, 'Let others shoot,
For here I leave my second leg,
    And the Forty-second Foot!'

The army-surgeons made him limbs:
    Said he, – 'They're only pegs:
But there's as wooden members quite
    As represent my legs!'

Now Ben he loved a pretty maid,
    Her name was Nelly Gray;
So he went to pay her his devours
    When he'd devoured his pay!

But when he called on Nelly Gray,
    She made him quite a scoff;
And when she saw his wooden legs,
    Began to take them off!

'O Nelly Gray! O, Nelly Gray!
    Is this your love so warm?
The love that loves a scarlet coat
    Should be more uniform!'

Said she, 'I loved a soldier once,
    For he was blithe and brave;

But I will never have a man
  With both legs in the grave!

'Before you had those timber toes,
  Your love I did allow,
But then, you know, you stand upon
  Another footing now!'

'O, Nelly Gray! O, Nelly Gray!
  For all your jeering speeches,
At duty's call, I left my legs
  In Badajos's *breaches*!'

'Why then,' said she, 'you've lost the feet
  Of legs in war's alarms,
And now you cannot wear your shoes
  Upon your feat of arms!'

'O, false and fickle Nelly Gray;
  I know why you refuse: —
Though I've no feet — some other man
  Is standing in my shoes!

'I wish I ne'er had seen your face;
  But, now, a long farewell!
For you will be my death; alas!
  You will not be my *Nell*!'

Now when he went from Nelly Gray,
  His heart so heavy got —
And life was such a burthen grown,
  It made him take a knot!

So round his melancholy neck,
  A rope he did entwine,

And, for his second time in life,
    Enlisted in the Line!

One end he tied around a beam,
    And then removed his pegs,
And, as his legs were off, – of course,
    He soon was off his legs!

And there he hung, till he was dead
    As any nail in town, –
For though distress had cut him up,
    It could not cut him down!

A dozen men sat on his corpse,
    To find out why he died –
And they buried Ben in four crossroads,
    With a *stake* in his inside!

members: M.P.'s
devours: *devoirs*, i.e. respects

THE BROKEN DISH

What's life but full of care and doubt,
 With all its fine humanities,
With parasols we walk about,
 Long pigtails and such vanities.

We plant pomegranate trees and things,
 And go in gardens sporting,
With toys and fans of peacock's wings
 To painted ladies courting.

We gather flowers of every hue,
 And fish in boats for fishes,
Build summer-houses painted blue –
 But life's as frail as dishes.

Walking about their groves of trees,
 Blue bridges and blue rivers,
How little thought them two Chinese,
 They'd both be smashed to shivers!

LOVE LANE

If I should love a maiden more,
And woo her every hope to drown,
I'd love her all the country o'er,
But not declare it out of town.

One even by a mossy bank,
That held a hornet's nest within,
To Ellen on my knees I sank —
How snakes will twine around the shin!

A bashful fear my soul unnerved,
And gave my heart a backward tug;
Nor was I cheered when she observed,
Whilst I was silent, — 'What a slug!'

At length my offer I preferred,
And Hope a kind reply forebode —
Alas the only sound I heard
Was, 'What a horrid ugly toad!'

I vowed to give her all my heart,
To love her till my life took leave,
And painted all a lover's smart —
Except a wasp gone up his sleeve!

But when I ventured to abide
Her father's and her mother's grants —
Sudden, she started up, and cried,
'Oh dear! I am all over ants!'

Nay, when beginning to beseech
The cause that led to my rebuff,

The answer was as strange a speech,
'A Daddy-Longlegs sure enough!'

I spoke of fortune – house – and lands,
And still renewed the warm attack, –
'Tis vain to offer ladies hands
That have a spider on the back!

'Tis vain to talk of hopes and fears
And hope the least reply to win,
From any maid that stops her ears
In dread of earwigs creeping in!

'Tis vain to call the dearest names
Whilst stoats and weazels startle by –
As vain to talk of mutual flames,
To one with glow-worms in her eye!

What checked me in my fond address,
And knocked each pretty image down?
What stopped my Ellen's faltering Yes?
A caterpillar on her gown!

To list to Philomel is sweet –
To see the Moon rise silver-pale, –
But not to kneel at Lady's feet
And crush a rival in a snail!

Sweet is the eventide, and kind
Its zephyr, balmy as the south;
But sweeter still to speak your mind
Without a chafer in your mouth.

At last emboldened by my bliss,
Still fickle Fortune played me foul,
For when I strove to snatch a kiss
She screamed — by proxy through an owl!

Then, Lovers, doomed to life or death
Shun moonlight, twilight, lanes, and bats,
Lest you should have in selfsame breath
To bless your fate — and curse the gnats!

Philomel: nightingale
chafer: beetle

PAIR'D *NOT* MATCH'D

Of wedded bliss
Bards sing amiss,
I cannot make a song of it;
For I am small,
My wife is tall,
And that's the short and long of it;

When we debate
It is my fate
To always have the wrong of it;
For I am small
And she is tall,
And that's the short and long of it!

And when I speak
My voice is weak,
But hers – she makes a gong of it;
For I am small,
And she is tall,
And that's the short and long of it;

She has, in brief,
Command in Chief,
And I'm but Aide-de-camp of it;
For I am small,
And she is tall,
And that's the short and long of it!

She gives to me
The weakest tea,
And takes the whole Souchong of it;
For I am small,

And she is tall,
And that's the short and long of it;

    She'll sometimes grip
    My buggy whip,
And make me feel the thong of it;
    For I am small,
    And she is tall,
And that's the short and long of it!

    Against my life
    She'll take a knife,
Or fork, and dart the prong of it;
    For I am small,
    And she is tall,
And that's the short and long of it!

    I sometimes think
    I'll take a drink,
And hector when I'm strong of it;
    For I am small,
    And she is tall,
And that's the short and long of it!

    O, if the bell
    Would ring her knell,
I'd make a gay ding dong of it;
    For I am small,
    And she is tall,
And that's the short and long of it!

THOMAS HOOD was born in 1799, the son of a London bookseller. Family circumstances obliged him to start work at the age of fourteen, as an office clerk. Later he worked as an engraver, and from 1821 until his death in 1845 he made a precarious living as a journalist, editor, poet and humorist. Several of his poems exposing social conditions have retained their power: notably 'The Song of the Shirt', which describes the miserable plight of seamstresses, and 'The Bridge of Sighs', a compassionate elegy for a young female suicide:

> Still, for all slips of hers,
> One of Eve's family.

And at least one of his more romantic poems, 'I remember, I remember', continues in popular favour. But today Hood is chiefly valued for his humorous verse, sometimes gently fanciful, sometimes satirical, often grotesque, and always rich in ingenious puns and parodies. It is this side of his work that has saved him from the fate foretold in the dedication to his first volume of comic verse, *Whims and Oddities*:

> What is a modern Poet's fate?
> To write his thoughts upon a slate:
> The Critic spits on what is done –
> Gives it a wipe – and all is gone.